Thorns On A Rose

Allexus Lopes

Presentation by *BookLeaf Publishing*

Web: www.bookleafpub.com

E-mail: info@bookleafpub.com

ISBN: 9789363305472

First edition 2024

To my children, Jesiah, Micah, Savyonna and Isaac. I love you! To my family who has always seen my talent. To my muse.

Thank You.

ACKNOWLEDGEMENT

Giving credit to life's greatest lesson.
People come and go.
I gained wisdom and experience.
It's meant to be fought for
And even sometimes letting go is an act of love
in itself.

PREFACE

Love brought you here. Get lost in the pages
with me.

Concrete Rose

Off the beaten path you find me
A Rose
With Thorns naturally
Beauty for the eyes to see.
I grew with the harsh elements
 Beating all the illusions
That nothing will come from this
I broke the mold
Showing life has begun.
I rose.

Soulmate

I want you after my heart and mind
I want you so intrigued by all the inner workings
of my thoughts,
that you get lost and forget that my body is
included in the deal.
I want you so taken back by the beauty my souls
light reveals, that you stand in awe of me when I
enter a room you are in.
My energy is contagious.
I want you touched by my aura before you crave
the touch of my hands.
Then I will know you are for me.

Love letter

I want to write you a love letter
Leave a kiss where I sign.
It will hold all of our secrets between the lines.
I want to write it with every intention of it being
my love spell.
As my words engage with your senses
You feel me.
Using my pen to glide across the paper
Like my fingers across your skin
Words come to me so effortlessly
Reminiscing the old
Manifesting our dreams
Our love will write itself in history
I can't wait for it to begin.

Yours

I want to be the woman who compliments your
whole existence
Not giving way to past tense or distance
I want to leave my soul tied around your finger
so you can't forget me
As my lips still linger across spaces of your
body that only God himself created for me
I want to be the woman who stumbles into your
arms leaving behind a mark that shows where I
come from
While holding your hand letting you be the man
who leads me into our future
I want to be the woman who drives you to
insanity when our paths can't meet
I want to dance through your memory skipping
to the beat of our favorite melodies
Leaving time at the doorstep
Locking out all that can't be manifested in our
beauty
I want to be the epitome of your being
As you toy with my persistence
Transferring energy through our fingertips
Fully trying to get a grip on all things worthy of
what we have created.

Through Space and Time

5

I'll hold space for you
I will walk away feeling an emptiness where you
should be
It's heartbreaking
Breathtaking
Necessary for our healing.
I will save room to cross paths
Once more in this lifetime
Wait to see who throws out a lifeline
Connected through energy
Experiencing this existence equally
I will hold space for the possibility
Welcoming all Good
Coming and Going

Trigger Warning

Please
Do not put me in a box
To perform at your leisure,
Taking my time and only shining when you say
to.
Don't compare me to another
And expect me to applaud and beg for you to
pick me.
There is no comparing.
I am not your trophy
But you will feel like you won the championship
once you have me.
I will not make it easy.
I put up walls,
No need for a fire breathing dragon
I spit fire when threatened.
You can't come to me as a victim of my crossfire
After creating this war between us.
I am always one to turn the other cheek
I will never look in that direction again
The damage is done, the person you knew is
gone.
I cannot help the ways I am triggered.
 I will not apologize for my actions
All I wanted was the satisfaction
of being understood.

Solitude

When night falls
That's when it all sinks in
The silence is so suffocating
Feeling the pressure
My chest tightens
My heart pounds
My thoughts go round and round
Loneliness is a constant reminder
The tears fall
The pain is sharp
I have been ripped apart
Reality only comes at night
Like a thief
Stealing what is left
Making me face the emptiness
In the dark I dwell
Facing my demons
Fighting hard to breathe
Fighting until morning.

Not My Love story

This chapter doesn't have you
I turned the pages
I reread every line
I'm not sure I like this story anymore
it definitely isn't mine.

I skipped to the ending
reading slow, thinking I missed your name.

I know I didn't miss how the writer describes
your face

clearly this is just a moment
you will return in the next chapters soon
because what kind of love story will this be if it
doesn't have you.

collateral damage

I am unable to undo this hurt that was caused
I just cant let it go.
it cut deep.
The dagger that was your words twisted as it
rammed into my ribs
piercing my lungs
I inhale
as the sting of knowing there is no return seeps
out of my bones.
this is the outcome
when hurt people try to love.
this is what pain feels like when the damage is
so bad it cant be undone

-leave me alone

generational curse

You tricked me
I followed you into the darkness
I held on tight
wanting only your light to guide me
hoping for your love
searching for your healing
only to be confronted by the reality of
nothingness
pain seething through its teeth
snatching the only memories I had left
reminding me I am a child of your trauma.
fooling me into thinking chaos was all I could
leave with.

old friends

I knew one day we would meet again
be in the same place at the same time
I knew one day I would meet your eyes as they
lock with mine
I knew one day would come
when we would know more than what we did
back then.
but will it make a difference?

Misery

12

NO
you cannot have it
This light is mine
I hold it tightly in my grasp
I know it's something you so desperately want to
have.
I cherish it with every fiber of my being.
you only want to destroy it.
to you that would be entertaining.
you creep closer
I wont let you steal what's inside of me
your demons will not terrorize me
just so you can have some company.

Bull in a china shop

13

You don't get to call me broken
when it was you who did the breaking.
I was whole when you found me.
I was bright,
but you wished me dull
I was strong but
each blow weakened my spirit.
I was fine china
as you crashed through me
leaving me in pieces.

Daydream

I found myself
Deep in thought
Flying through other dimensions
you take place in.
I seen us in other lifetimes
I recognized your soul.
I fast forward to our golden years
where you and I are gray and old.
I traveled back and forth for a while
Taking in small details we usually forget
I breathe you In and my heart smiles
my senses heighten when I get near you.
I feel a rush through my body as I realize
I was lost in a daydream
my reality doesn't include you.

April Showers

it rained in my head for so long
my judgement clouded
my feelings rising fast, I was drowning.
flash floods
sweeping away any sense I have left
clearly this storm is too big for me.
my heart boomed loud in my ears
like thunder rolling by
the shock of it all
has me stuck in place
as I watch the spark I once had leave my eyes.
I prayed for the sun.
begging for just one bright day
I just needed the calm to come
I wanted to hear the whispers of the winds song.
THIS TO SHALL PASS
soon I will witness the flowers
after the rain is gone.

What I know now

I wish I could see me
all versions of myself.
I wish I could love them all then
because I do now.
I wish I could forgive myself, but I just didn't
know how.
not knowing I would bloom and find a way out.
I wish I could tell that girl she was beautiful
I wish I knew how much power and beauty my
soul holds.
my strength came from my struggle
If only I felt that then.
I wouldn't have been so broken.
- I am enough.

where did it all go wrong

wrong place, wrong time ?
too many variables
too many impossibles to be possible
too hard, too much
but was it?
was it really love ?
was it our need of something
anything to feel.
feelings were so deep
too deep for our souls to handle
where do we go from here ?
-i need you still

win some, lose some

Not all losses are the same
some build you
make you stronger
make you get up and fight again
there is better
you just have to keep pushing
past the struggle,
the negativity
and get over the fear of losing.
some things aren't meant to be kept
longer than a season
know that there is always a window
when all doors have been closed
what you will gain in the end will only be for
you!
You will WIN

Be Different! Love, Mom

I want to tell you all about the world
and what it has been to me
I wish I could elaborate without tarnishing your
reality
the world takes more than it gives
it has not been kind to my spirit
I have so much light I have given
and it has lashed its anger In my direction in
order to dim it
I wish I could tell you that its beauty outweighs
the ugly that consumes it
but I won't.
I cant lie to you and shield you from its
atrocities
I wish I could explain this in a way that doesn't
scare you into not living
truth is life doesn't give us a choice
we fight hard to get up
as it knocks us down more and more
so let me tell you what you can be to the world
be the light in someones darkest moments
be the change that is needed
be what you have always wanted and keep
loving
because you are what the world is missing.

True Love , My Child

I love the way the light catches in your eyes
I see glimmers of meant to be's and happiness
whenever you smile
I love hearing music when you speak
knowing every octave is In perfect harmony
I love how my heart recognizes yours
knowing there is no other I could imagine loving
more.
I love how each moment of my day seems to
include you.
knowing our connection is on another level
feeling as though maybe our souls have been
tied to FOREVER
I LOVE YOU

Your Rose

You planted your seed
watered it daily
Spoke so highly of its beauty
Provided sunlight as needed
Always being careful
Over time you watched the climate change
and your Rose would wilt
But you stayed constant
Offering daily affirmation
no matter the weather
You would watch this rose grow and bloom
Even when you would bleed from her thorns
You loved harder and continued to sprinkle her
petals
gently letting it trickle into her roots
Always knowing that this Rose was rare and
resilient to change
Standing tall
adding to the beauty of your life.

9 789363 305472